HEALTH, WEALTH, LOVE, BEAUTY & HARMONY

Karen A. Gravit

InfusedMedia Co. LLC
www.infusedmedia.co
1-888-251-6088

CONTENTS

ACKNOWLEDGMENTS

To my daughters who have always been true to me and to my good friend who led me to the Five Rites.

FOREWORD

Though I cannot guarantee anyone's success, I am confident that I have been given better all-around help than anything else found, especially in the area of health. Proven more than once in its ability to greatly transform health and other areas of my life, the Universal Power, what I call the UP, is rebuilding my life and helping me find true whole well-being through the Five Rites. Unrivalled by anything I have ever experienced before, this quintessential guidance to insightful help is empowering my life by lifting me up out of the ruts as I write this book.

The first five chapters define each symbol's significant meaning for each rite, describe my own progress through each rite, and give an account of how each one has empowered my life in a real way as they are easily incorporated into daily living in order to help the reader to see how effortless and worthwhile they are. The last chapter illustrates how all five areas evolve for greater empowerment in a continual cycle occurring just like the natural cycles of the world; showing their simple yet complex orderly function for whole well-being. I do not give the actual directions for the Five Rites since there are books and other online resources that give detailed instructions. Instead, I am revealing what I have intuitively learned and openly experienced in an informative, neutral way to encourage each individual to find their own one-on-one guidance through a unique quest as the rites are continued. It should be understood that only through the individual's inner guidance that one's life can be holistically improved in the most beneficial way creating communal harmony since each life is unique even though universally connected. Not being religious or trying to force my beliefs about GOD on anyone, I much rather ask that everyone follows their own intuitive guidance to the Universal Power, the UP, as I did to come to a closer extraordinary relationship that is better understood and more appreciably followed for truly satisfying results.

While performing each exercise rite, it's equally important to focus on where each energy center is located physically to greatly influence physical and inner areas if a desired improvement is to be seen and experienced. The revisions have been added due to my further learning after the first year of implementing the rites back into my life. No longer allowing annoying obstacles or negativity to keep me from reaching a full potential existence, I am able to go deeper for a more complete picture.

Before starting these exercises it's advisable to check with your physician, especially when any medical conditions are present or if you haven't exercised in a while. These five rites are more of an exercise to activate the major energy centers along the spine up to the top of the head and are not for everyone because of their powerful effects. However, they are very helpful if tolerated to keep the energy centers running efficiently as the body ages so that the body and mind stays as youthful as possible.

INTRODUCTION

Growing up and feeling good about my true self, a bit shy but desiring friends, I was deeply disheartened to get a lot of very negative, tense actions and reactions from others that tried to goad me to unkind behavior. Seeing nothing wrong with choosing to be upright, which originated from my inner connection to the UP and encouraged by upright adults around me, I was teased a lot because I was quiet and stable. Then, later on in my youth when provocation escalated, I strongly turned inward to the Universal Power (UP), whom I deeply sensed to be the true inner strength of my whole being, healing my wounds and guiding me to higher attainment while empowering my life.

But, after leaving home post high school and relentlessly going my own way for 30 years, I found myself needing out of a forlorn relationship and isolated from the outside world while being a full-time mother. Being given an inner warning that it would not be easy to go back out into the world again, I found myself easily, but strangely welcomed into a provocative crowd due to promoting my newly attained, muscularly-sculpted body. Depressed and upset over the years wasted in marriage without intimacy, I therefore followed the advice of a new found friend that I was easily influenced by and went through with an act of dissipation even though inwardly warned not to do because of harassment that would follow. Finally after being misunderstood and mistreated in almost all relationships as well as the workplace, I once again reached up for the trusted UP's help and took a critical step that was inwardly forewarned to be harshly criticized by the outside world, however definitely required to ultimately push me in the right direction.

When all kinds of trouble suddenly disrupted my life, I recalled near the end of the 1st round of youthful torment how I was inwardly foretold of a more serious time that I would face. Seeing how the 2nd round escalated with more animosity and similar but more intense attacks than seen in the 1st round, I knew that the outrageous situation was not a fluke. Deeply desiring to be a real, contributing part of the outside world, but being left out in the cold, I have kept persevering through my trust in the UP that has thoroughly sustained me. Then, I was intuitively empowered to understand my cooperative responsibility to personally endure this hardship of seclusion and scorn in order to completely connect so that I would find the solution for dissolving the disruption in my life and others through pure, sound guidance.

After I actively began to follow the intuitive help to research my worsening health, I was inwardly guided to supportive basic information first and then methodically and ultimately led to the Five Tibetan Rites that started my deeper quest for a constructive way to real harmony within and around me. This orderly balance was properly organizing all of my gained knowledge and understanding of the body, mind, and spirit into a powerful, sound method that would disintegrate all road blocks in the way of success. With escalating antagonism, I deeply meditated upon the stabilizing life energy that cleared my mind so that new, constructive thoughts were imagined as I drew a simple symbol for the movement of each rite in its order so as to internally see and understand them as a unit without added distractions. Sketching these symbols in the sand every day while performing the rites, I sensed that there was a more meaningful depth to these well-balanced, aesthetically flowing symbols involving more than just health. Further outside strife generated more creative determination to find the rightful meanings to these symbols. Ultimately, through an optimistic search for words to a joyful melody that flowed through my being as I assuredly sensed that good things would advance through the creative life energy flow of the rites, a beautiful quintet cheerfully emerged. Immediately, I knew that I had the exact words and order as they flowed together in perfect harmony and rhyme to my powerful melody.

Later on, after perceiving how the harmoniously flowing words, (Health Wealth Love Beauty Harmony) matched the exact order of the deeply inspired symbols giving them their intrinsic meanings, an equally powerful confirmation came that night as I engaged in a celebratory stroll along a dark, empty beach walkway and graciously stared up at the clear, starry expanse. While gazing into the night sky as I used to growing up in the country where the stars were clear to see, a tremendous awe of how small I was in comparison to the heavens above would rouse my desire to connect to the powerful creator of this astronomical magnitude in a revering intuitive way. For many prior months, while curiously studying the bright star to the north, my attention was directed to the stars aligned with it, and at this specific time I was stunned to see four stars aligned with the northern bright star to my right as they were positioned over the ocean. Strongly sensing that they were depicting the five drawn symbols with the middle star having a warmer glow, which portrayed the Love Embrace symbol, I intuitively felt that this stellar event was congratulating me on finding the key elements to the harmonized communal search.

Furthermore, this thrilling confirmation was encouragement to continue uncovering its enriching depths, with thoughts immersed in daily meditation, writing down anything insightfully interesting that would give needed proof and real help to others as well as for myself. Showing up with orderly balance, each layer was revealed to bring more understanding as the life energy stirred my body and relit creative imagination. Searching for an overall name for the five meanings, I continued meditating on this deep balanced system to unravel more of what I sensed it was all about.

While looking at the meanings of each rite, I glanced at the first letter of each one and suddenly the idea came to sound them out phonetically. To my delight, exactly like the harmonious flow of the words to the melody out of my mouth rolled, "whole well-being".

Even though my attempts to strive for love and harmony have been discouraging, my fire of self-esteem has been satisfyingly rekindled, favorably supplied, vibrantly fanned, and energetically increased by the influential help of the five rites. As a compilation of difficult issues kept my life below the satisfactory line, I became more determinately focused to terminate the worsening 2nd round of harassing events and was intuitively guided by the higher power and ultimately channeled into the right corner pocket of success. Now I'm no longer smothered by disharmony as I continue on the path to the highest good possible.

CHAPTER 1

<u>Health Spin</u>

The cells are energetically restored and refreshed as they are spun into healthy action forcing out congestion and creating full life.

1. Symbol's Meaning

The symbol O illustrates the body's motion as it spins around in a circle while performing the 1st rite, named the Health Spin, and refers to the 1st and 2nd energy centers, which is the area of basic survival located in the base of the spine and the area of satisfaction and emotions located in the sacral spine, respectively. The symbol also signifies the letter O in origin, which relates to the beginning of new life in this book, and further verifies that health is foremost important in the whole well-being balance just like I was given the insight when desiring to achieve true harmony before this search began. It also resembles the shape of a healthy cell, which is the basic building block of the body that is strong enough to keep the body in balance.

Spinning to the right activates the spinning wheels of all the energy centers so that they too spin in the correct clockwise motion and gradually increase their synchronized spin, just like any coordinated flow that begins to move unhampered. This activation of the energy centers keeps the areas that they govern in healthy motion so that everything flows in optimal balance. Therefore, any blockages in the energy centers should be eliminated due to the powerfully energetic flow so that more youthfully vibrant health, and ultimately, a pleasantly stable whole well-being should be possible.

2. Health Spin Rite

Being a bit off balanced in the beginning, I noticed that a better way to balance when spinning was to take small steps in one place with the right foot and take larger steps with the left for the outer circumference of the spin circle. With arms held horizontally out and palms down, relaxing the shoulders and knees while keeping the spine in a safe neutral position, a more controlled circle was created, which made it easier to breathe and I was able to turn with faster momentum keeping my gaze downward while counting a fixed marker to complete the set amount of spins. Starting with 3 spins at first, I was up to the maximum 21 within the first week maybe because I used to love spinning when I was a child.

At first when I began the rites, experiencing discomfort in the lower left abdominal area created a feeling somewhat like suction pulling upward and outward as if harmful, unhealthy material was being vacuumed out. Blockages in the energy centers were possibly why the light-headedness was experienced, but this uneasiness dissipated together with the health problems. In addition, being barefoot helped to ground and stabilize my body as well as initially feel the life energy in the feet so that I could feel the whirlwind stir the grounded soles increasing its intensity as it moved all the way up to the top of my head, especially when I'm able to spin in a fast, tight circle. Gaining momentum as the energy climbed upward, it felt as if I was being elevated off the ground by the rush of energy started from the innermost areas to the outermost electrifying the cells to the point that

I could feel body fluid being pulled upward and outward, especially in the torso giving the chest, shoulders and arms a gentle stretch, as well as the head clearing my mind while forcing out stagnant toxic waste.

Coming back again after leaving the rites tucked away on the shelf,there are times of not feeling well or tired that I usually need to spin at a lower speed while looking at a landmark, and then speed up near the end when my balance is better. Afterwards, I keep my arms out for stability and in case I start to fall, or bring my hands up to my head and squat down until I feel stable. With more experience, I am noticing how relaxed normal breathing during and after the spin helps to clear away the light-headedness while stimulating life energy deep inside. Eventually, whatever was causing the awkwardness will be spun out by the efficient life energy flow through the energy centers and I will again experience benefits in the way of leaps and bounds.

3. My Health Spin Experience

Health being the most important when I was given insight to the order in which my life would be improved after searching for a way out of the deep disorder largely by acting on others advice. Seeing how the word heal is first and main part of word health, I now perceive that health relates more to the on-going process of healing rather than the healthy state as status quo, especially when I've been healed of a variety of ailments all through my past.

Now as I'm emotionally reminded of my dad telling me how health is so important and necessary in order to truly enjoy life, so therefore, to always make health a priority, it was at the time that he was dying of cancer. Although it was not known to me or my siblings how ill he was until it was too late, I have always felt and presently feel a great responsibility for forging a new complete way to whole well-being that naturally creates vibrant health, especially with so many in need along with my own recent experience with serious health issues.

Before the beginning of the 2nd round of chaos, I sensed that it would not be as easy to regain my health the next time that illness brought me down as I began to gain muscle and see a stronger, youthfully lean body emerge from a disciplined diet and workout schedule. After experiencing pain in the lower left abdominal area and researching Diethylstilbestrol (DES) exposure (in utero), I sensed that there was more to the problem than a small ovarian cyst which was diagnosed after getting a second opinion from a specialist. Dismissing the medical doctors' conclusion that the cyst was nothing to worry about as the area of concern seemed to be growing larger and was becoming more painful, I was certain that the needed solution wasn't to be found in any ordinary approach, but instead it would involve a deeper, all-encompassing search using the intuitive wisdom of the higher power.

Unsure where to begin searching and feeling depressingly powerless, I experienced the following:

- Body bulking up and losing its slender, muscular definition and skin becoming more pale, sun-sensitive and inflamed
- Increasing pallor, swelling of painful gums in my mouth along with fading lip color that was looking as pale as my skin
- Swollen veins especially noticeable at the wrist, top of hands and at the ankles with noticeable edema
- Unusual menstrual bleeding with increasing exhaustion and painful pressure in the lower left abdomen where I palpated a moveable mass
- Light-headedness and depressive, confused thinking

When I focused more on weight lifting to go into a physically demanding career, my body was transformed by strong muscles that were more aesthetic, but being told by body building judges that my lower body didn't match my more defined upper body, I became further concerned about the bulging abdomen because I had a really defined set of abs. Intuitively sensing an inner warning that my somewhat healthier weightlifter body was very temporary because of the looming unhealthy conditions as well as dissatisfaction with my whole life situation; I sensed the tough, disciplined road that I would have to take in order to find the balanced solution and that it would catch up with me eventually. Getting hints that I was chubby from a personal trainer whom I would see at the strand by the beach like when he asked if the vertical bulges on either side of my spine were fat.

Then the arrival of forewarned ill-health came three years later when I started experiencing worse conditions of the following:

- Decreased strength when working out with my usual amount of weight and feeling more distress from lactic acid buildup
- Looking more like the unhealthy weightlifter as the abdominal area bulged out more unsightly in my snug fitting outfits along with increased overall inflammation causing my muscle definition to disappear under what looked like an increasing layer of fat but was more likely the buildup of toxic edema
- Distorting and aging inflammation in my facial area, especially noticeable around the eyes making me look exhaustively ill and more unfamiliar to myself with signs of a double chin and moon face
- Noticeable swelling in fingers as my rings were becoming uncomfortably tight along with hands

becoming irritated with noticeable redness and itchy tingling sensations
- White coarse hair growing in, particularly in the frontal area that was becoming sparse
- More light-headedness and exhaustion especially before and during uterine bleeding that were more severe in pain and blood flow with unusual material
- More depression and confused decision making
- Prehypertension and raised cholesterol level above 200

However, taking time off from working out, I felt even more exhaustion, and found it difficult to even do short five minute, light workouts that would normally be easy for me. After giving doctors one last chance at the advice of a current acquaintance and realizing that their shallow hunt and peck method was not going to bring a helpful solution to this worsening life-encompassing problem, I decided not to waste any more time and money on this approach. Seeing the same, slow, incomplete diagnosis of my condition as before, I recalled how I was helped in a more wonderful, complete way when I was very young.

Releasing my complicated health problem completely, I desperately sought the help of the UP through meditation and prayer as I had done before. For instance, many times as a child I would be too sick to go outside and play, and one night I felt recurrently nauseated. So, my dad told me to close my eyes and think of good things like being outside and feeling the fresh air on my face. With my eyes closed while meditating on these thoughts, I felt the power of the UP bring me loving peace and I was able to release the tense, nauseated feelings and relax as I fell asleep believing that I would feel better in the morning. Then I slept through the whole night and woke up restored knowing that a powerful restoration had occurred. With this observation, I also began to meditate at night while resting on my back lying straight as possible while falling asleep and thinking about becoming stronger and healthier in order to fearlessly play with my friends.

The results of meditating on the UP and releasing my sickness worked out better than any help from medicine or chicken soup so-to-speak and quicker. I recall when I recovered from a very serious sickness too fast for my mother who was either disappointed or perplexed that I felt strong enough to go outside and play so soon. Even more puzzling to my parents as well was how I did not need a jacket to keep warm when the Midwest evenings would turn cold as I stayed outside after dark to play. Through my new inner strength, I began doing pull-ups and twirling on the parallel bars as well as running faster than any of my brothers or playmates that tried to run after me and was no longer teased about being a weakling. Using this inner strength, I placed first every time, even lapping some competitors, except for a few mishaps, in the mile-run within my school's district area and also qualified for state finals all four years of high school.

Now back to the present, after getting nowhere with the last doctor visit and completely surrendering my concerns to the munificent UP vowing to seek complete guidance, I woke up from a very restful night's sleep and was given clear directions to start eating a diet of high antioxidants and cut way back on meat sources of protein. Within the next week, I was fortuitously given more direct guidance to specific antioxidants as I randomly came across an infomercial that I quickly glanced at while flipping through other TV programs, but then went back to after sensing something significantly important about its health benefits. Interesting to note how this was the only time that I had downtime after arriving at the current job. Otherwise, due to having no other source to view this wide variety of television channels, I would not have seen the needed catalyst that convinced me to stay with complete natural, healthy food sources as much as possible in addition to a powerful antioxidant drink.

Once I incorporated the quality antioxidants into my daily diet, the exhausted, nauseated feeling dissipated and I slightly felt more energy. Surprisingly, I also quickly acquired a taste for this veggie, anti-oxidant variety over the more bland, meaty diet that I was on before. Sensing the necessary cleansing of toxins that the flavorful phytonutrient nourishment provided, less than a month later, pressure felt in my left ovarian area was relieved with a sudden flow of dark blood from my uterus. In addition, the increasingly painful lumps that were felt in the lateral sides of my breasts were deflated and undetected in a rescheduled appointment for an alternative ultrasound that I had insisted on instead of another mammogram to thoroughly detect any abnormalities.

With some strength, I began light workouts in order to regain my aesthetic figure, but instead, more pain especially in the lower abdomen along with muscle weakness and depletion resulted in a more disappointing, bloated body. Inwardly prompted about my deteriorating dental health and amalgam fillings, I soon received another warning when a friend told me about a member of church who experienced mercury toxicity and pointed her out to me. Seeing her swollen face, especially around the eyes, reminded me of my own facial distortion. The dentist exam conclusion was that I had gum disease that would not get better and disclaimed the health concern about amalgam fillings. However after the dentist replaced a decayed metal filling deep inside the back wisdom tooth with the new composite filling that I agreed with, the area around the tooth immediately felt less pain and I was able to reach around it easier with the toothbrush. Within a couple days, a bout of intense menstrual cramps brought out a small piece of spongy tissue relieving the painful pressure in the lower abdomen, but more erratically unusual menstrual bleeding occurred with massive amounts of strange tissue being expelled. Shortly after this, white course hair that appeared only in the front part of my scalp began to fall out mocking the side effects of cancer treatments.

Something was definitely wrong when I began feeling deep, sharp pain that would radiate down from the left hip and painful mental disorientation when I would be awakened at night or when first waking up in the morning (like my brain was sizzling as I heard a strange hissing sound). Beginning to think that this health problem was spreading, I sensed a stronger hunch to get the other dental fillings replaced. Finally researching mercury toxicity signs and symptoms, I then noted that I had experienced many of them since first having metal amalgam fillings put in my teeth. Obeying the hunch to replace the remaining fillings with composite fillings, even though expensive and not in my budget, was helpful advice as any further delay would have been more expensive due to soon losing insurance coverage when a sudden layoff occurred just a few months later. Also, further delay would have been more detrimental, because of the increasing pain and inflammation in the lower jaw that had recently caused my gums to split in the worst affected area below a molar extensively filled. Even though the dentist detected no decay in the amalgam fillings during scheduled checkups, he then discovered some degree of decay underneath each one when removing them.

Then a week after all the metal fillings were replaced, I was abruptly awakened in the middle of the night from a sudden deluge of menstrual blood that relieved the building painful pressure in my lower abdomen soaking my heavy sweatpants that I had fallen asleep in because I was too exhausted to change out of. Following this event, within a month, I had a major uterine cleansing after a mass that I had palpated in the left ovary area slowly moved down to the uterus and felt like a water balloon bouncing inside when I walked around. Suddenly intense labor-like pain resulted in an uncomfortable mass exiting the uterus through the vaginal canal which brought immediate relief from pressure in the lower abdomen and lower back and giving my cumbersome middle a lighter feeling. A couple days later, measurements revealed a 5 pound weight loss and 2 inch loss around the waist. Even with this huge cleansing, more dysmenorrhea continued along with further bulging pressure in the abdomen in addition to sudden slippage in the lumbar spinal column while walking continued for months that turned into years. Later, I began noticing emaciated areas in the face, finger pads, chest, and buttocks that made me look like a cancer patient when the toxic inflammation left along with less muscle mass. Sadly reminded of losing my parents to cancer-related deaths after they had lived stressful lives, deeply motivated I reached up to the Universal Power for trusting help to end this life-draining ailment that I sensed was meant for me to endure emotionally in order to focus on a complete solution that relieves health problems and lessens stressful feelings that I was now experiencing as outside sources of harassment began to show up in my all-ready troubled life.

Once again, given inner guidance as more receptive intuition is gained, I was actively led to precise information on a natural herbal treatment for female dysmenorrhea helping to end the chronic condition that proved to be life-saving and better than everyday advice that seems blasé' when it comes to actually being healed. Further guidance to read about other alternative treatments, like transcendental meditation (TM), gave me insightful understanding that I was being methodically led toward the ultimate solution that would definitely be evident once I touched upon it. Sometime later, a weekly telephone discussion with my friend brought up my recently started exercise for relaxation and toning that suddenly caused her to look at the bookcase alongside her desk and look directly at the book about the Five Tibetan Rites, of which she immediately told me about. Sensing the importance, the next day I went to the library and found online printable instructions and then gave them a try as soon as I was able to get to the gym. Even though I was very inflexible and awkward while trying them at first like many new exercises feel, the stimulating energy was felt deep within my joints, muscles and nerves as if I had received a jump start back to life out of a semi-conscious state of anesthesia from the powerful awakening of life energy flowing within me. My mind was also deeply awakened from depressively cloudy thinking to more clear awareness of what was going on inside and outside of my body unlike anything that I had ever experienced before.

A flashback of performing similar exercises brought back recollections of being shown how to do the rites in the basement of my parents' house by a visitor that I never saw again. Being very young at the time, I don't remember why I stopped practicing them, but I do recall the powerful sensation felt in and around me as well as the deeper discernment that was overwhelming when I would sense the tense feelings of adults in my presence. Shortly after the first introduction to the rites, my life changed with a move to a small town and a larger house, my own room, and a much larger property with our own woods to explore, as if it may have been my subconscious dream come to life. However the 1st round started up some years later around puberty when teasing began and then escalated most likely due to poor self-esteem, but then it started the desire to open up my awareness to the Universal Power in an amazing way that I would draw upon for strength and wisdom.

Now back to the present, a very powerful storm blew through the area during the first week of February when I started practicing the rites. Besides being strong enough to blow most of the leaves of a young tree onto my car that I had parked next to, the storm also dropped the first noticeable precipitation in the area during the drought-ridden normal rainy season and began the start of cloudy, wet conditions that lasted most of the year which was unusual for the southern area's ordinary hot, sunny summer climate. Other unusual phenomena that arose while performing the rites also showed me their energetic influence, such as a sudden increase of the wind that was hardly noticeable moments before, or the time when inwardly guided to a place on the beach and momentarily gazing up at a small, lonely cloud above me before beginning the rites, only to look up again when performing the 3rd rite, the Love Embrace, to see that the little cloud had grown into a large circle of clouds that resembled the earth. Suddenly the wind picked up and by the time I had finished the rites, the clouds were spread out into a long strand of separated clouds along the coast to end up as an electrifying sunset to gaze upon as I left. Another rare occurrence happened twice on separate days and different times when intensely practicing the rites at different spots on the beach, when a group of dolphins showed up to frolic for a while in the waves near to my location, and then continued on their way as I finished the rites. Even though these rare events seemed to occur at the beginning when a lot of blockages were being cleared out of the energy centers, I still notice the wind pick up many times while practicing them. Recently witnessing a powerful thunderstorm that lashed out until the early hours before dawn while I concentrated on the energy flow that continued after finishing the rites and staying up all night to do revisions on this book, I still had more energy than the day before.

Obviously the Five Rites have brought tremendously better health as I see the extensively toxic infection that was throughout my body empty out leaving a slimmer, strong body glowing with resiliently supple skin, and equipped with underlying sharp senses of touch, smell, taste, hearing and sight topped with an intuitively greater understanding of the whole well-being connection to the higher power for best possible health on the path of healing. Guided to more natural, peaceful atmospheres that are filled with stimulating energy, I'm able to benefit from the enriching rewards of greatly improved life energy that brings creativity to the whole picture. Securely confident that this universal life energy is unstoppable by any horrific interference, I look beyond the worsening, finite world and meditate on the infinite, inner connection coming into clearer vision. For I am certain that this vigorously improved health, energetically created by connecting to the universal power that flows all around us and through us, is only the beginning. I am sure to see all energy center areas similarly improved if allowed to by this method that balances the whole being.

Experiencing the following exuberantly better-than-expected results within one year of starting the Five Rites:

- Resilient, taut, youthful, supple skin with radiant color, especially improved in nail beds and lips plus a more youthful looking face that I once knew
- Healthy, firm gums with good color and no more deep pockets, or irritation especially when brushing
- Abdominal area well defined (not seen since pre-pregnancy years) with inner core strength that kicks into high gear when exercising after clearing out of toxins and blockages in the area that caused a bulging, painfully weak abdomen and lower back
- More youthfully toned and muscularly balanced than the weightlifter body that needs no filler, tuck, or lift with workouts that are less time consuming using bodyweight and resistance in practical exercises that

strengthen the whole body for everyday routine and above

- Improved muscle strength and definition and more stable joints with little stiffness or soreness as if I am working with a youthful body again without constant shoulder pain that was previously felt
- Tight, healthy veins with normal blood pressure and cholesterol levels
- Healthy hair growth especially in the area that was coarse and sparse
- Feeling constant renewed vigor as the spinning wheels have increased so noticeably that they seem to lift me up as I effortlessly glide up steep hills and whiz along energetically on walks that used to be exhausting and draining
- Steady energy all day long, even when getting less than normal amount of sleep without the need for a nap
- Mental clarity and alertness with all senses improved
- Inner contentment that everything is going to be alright

Blockages in the 1st and 2nd energy centers can cause illness in the reproductive system, liver and pancreas such as cancer and can also create emotional upset, which were also exacerbated by external sources of physical and emotional harassment. Though negatively affecting me, the outside actions positively increased my passion to connect to the higher power for needed help and the increased flow of life energy through the energy centers from the five rites helped improve both my physical and mental health while giving my intuitive psyche a tune-up and disciplined workout.

As the flow of life energy clears the blockages in the root and sacral areas, unhealthy conditions dissipate as I also experience good emotions that bring stability and a secure feeling of where I'm at with passion to explore the path of higher knowledge, especially for the deeper benefits of the Five Rites that have given me a healthier body and better emotionally balanced life. With all the energy centers being spun into the right direction, negativity no longer delays or upsets my intended purpose as the presentation of anymore obstacles becomes obedient learning steps to accomplish tasks proficiently with understanding that by allowing this energetic process to clear negative blocks out of the way, I receive more benefits in the health and wealth areas.

Now that I have been inwardly guided away from the coast to a more peaceful and intriguing place, I am richly rewarded as I get back to my grass roots in fervent pastures with a greater intuitive understanding of nature. Performing the rites as the wind suddenly picks up during a calm day gives me a reassuring message of future rewards to come as new, healthier life continues to flow into me through the universal life energy that relaxes my whole being. Always desiring to bring balance to whatever is uneven, with math being one of my favorites, this phenomenal discovery has been challenging and tough, but necessary and rewarding, vigorously improving healthy balance and harmony in a wildly, bewildered world, the natural energy flow of the Five Tibetan Rites have aroused my universal life energy.

CHAPTER 2

Wealth Cup

Reaching up in disciplined effort to receive required power energizes the Wealth Cup's confidence for orderly upward flow of all energy centers to reach highest possible potential

1. Symbol's Meaning

The symbol U illustrates the position of the body as it works to flex in order to bring the legs and head up in the 2nd rite, named the Wealth Cup, and refers to the 3rd energy center, which is the area of willpower, desire and fire of individual confidence, located in the upper abdominal area of the solar plexus. The symbol signifies the letter U in union, which is the inner being connection to the UP, for a definite personal image, positively motivated, for the united, most beneficial purpose. As the body actively flexes and this area is concentrated upon, the life energy builds and motivates out to actively energize the other areas to manifest their purpose. Similarly, the symbol represents the way a cell's binding site opens up to bring in needed substances, like in active transport where energy is needed. So, like in active transport, the Wealth Cup takes unified effort of the abdominal muscles along with the whole body and mind to reach up in the flexed position and then back with orderly disciplined effort for powerful drive that brings in desired energy for overall success. The flexed upward position also resembles the shape of a universal plug that allows one to plug into the available energy supply anywhere in the world, therefore the Wealth Cup allows anyone to plug into the limitless Universal Power for the real powered-up fire of individual will that not only creates real inner contentment, but universally unified contentment. Summarily, the 2nd rite movement to reach up and stretch out is the same way that all the rites move to receive the life energy.

2. Wealth Cup Rite

At first, when beginning to perform the 2nd rite, my weakened body, especially the abdomen and lower back, was uncomfortably stiff and uncoordinated as I struggled with the flexing motion. Keeping my knees bent instead of straight at the beginning of the exercise, and then raising my legs to rise up in fully flexed position helped to take pressure off of the lower back, lowering back down to bent knees at the end of the exercise. With effort to focus on improving the abdominal strength while maintaining correct body position, the awkwardness and discomfort decreased while the abdominal strength increased and muscular body heat spread out to all other areas. Simultaneously feeling more coordinated strength throughout the body, the necessary, disciplined effort was worth the manifested rewards as I finally executed the 2nd rite's complete movement with confident skill and power. Whenever I feel rushed or tired, I decrease the repetitions of the exercise and also found that using a yoga-type mat helps keep the body stable and in one place so that I didn't have to stop and reposition myself.

Finally, with increased abdominal and inner core strength, my whole body is more stable in its movement of all the rites, and thus a better physical performance of combined disciplined effort that increases the life energy flow into each energy center. Clearing blockages has resulted in better health in the Wealth Cup area by forcing out harmful toxins that caused abdominal pain when doing any abdominal workouts and alleviate any other trunk problems, especially when getting up or down.

3. My Wealth Cup Experience

The Wealth Cup rite is not as fun as the Health Spin because it takes self-control to rise up, but it's a necessary part of the balanced order that fires up the life purpose bringing meaning to existence. Just as I was intuitively told that it would not be easy to go after this search for harmony, I was not told that it would be impossible. Therefore, with continued disciplined effort to reach up and stretch out instead of giving up or in, I am more in synch with the inner self that is quietly guided by the UP who gently shows how to create harmonious balance within and with such, I am able to mirror the same harmony with others using the discipline learned within this 2nd rite.

With the disciplined effort of this rite helping to accomplish difficult tasks, being inwardly coaxed to give up most processed foods because of my decreased finances, I was able to cut back on the expensive bag habit. Reminded of how I was disciplined to eat necessary, nutritious food while growing up during the recession, similar rationing now has helped me to create strong, healthy muscle tone just as in my youth. Helping to make the right decisions in the health area concerning survival, stability, and satisfaction in the emotional area of relationships, desires, and creativity, I have been guided to a more enriching environment to enjoy nature again and find a worthwhile path to well-being.

Near the beginning of the uprooting of what I thought was a decently stable life that I was trying to hold on to and improve, confused and dismayed at the chain of events upsetting my stability, I was forced to give up some of my more valued material things sitting in storage. Hoping that this would be just a temporary uprooting and reorganization was the biggest mistake because I now understand how I was being disciplined and warned to give up bad habits that were keeping me from true harmony and that this struggle would only continue once rooted again if I did not make a hard, right choice to give up unnecessary items and desires. After the shock and heartache, I was gratefully relieved of the stress and came to realize that more valuable, meaningful treasures would replace what I had sacrificed. Sure enough, after enduring many hard years of having less of everything except work, the disciplined effort has easily aided my relocation making it a smooth transition. Experiencing continual healing, my newly gratifying desire to seek rare, beautiful experiences is priceless compared to the momentary enjoyment that came from the superficial, mundane drama that left a deep rut of unhappiness over time. Now, I am no longer swayed by the trifle, absurd attempts to make one's life seem more exciting and important only to sacrifice true contentment and cherished moments.

Trying to find self-worth and meaningful purpose on my rightful path, this methodical guidance to sound accurate knowledge has cut out the wasteful energy of rushing after a selfish pursuit and ending up further back and worse off than at the beginning. At first, disappointed being overlooked in the workplace or making the wrong decisions about what career path to pursue, the continued all-out effort to use my full potential while at the bottom, just as in the flexing done in the Wealth Cup rite, increased my work ethic, thus quality and output. As a result, my increased unified desire actively propelled my path down its intended beneficial route for rewarding accomplishments beneficial to complete harmony. Now it's evident that everything has worked out for the entire good as all the skills acquired from various prior jobs are implemented to accomplish the current demanding daily tasks with a fired up willpower to easily overcome the frustrating distractions and problems. In addition, past employment misfortunes and financial losses were beneficial in order to break out from the unfulfilling grind and gain self-honor through harrowing hard work that increased my personal power in relation to the world empowering the potential to securely sew up present projects.

The repeated effort of the Wealth Cup's flexing action gave me the overall compassion to forgive and tolerate the cruelty directed at me again and again while feeling pain in the abdomen with each repetition as I used disciplined controlled acceptance by reaching up for intelligent support. With an understanding of the importance of self-control to unite the energy centers, continued discipline directed up toward the love area that confidently soothed my nerves, my trust in the authority of the divine power brought comfort and relief along with desire to live truly at peace with self and others, much like the abdominal muscles brought orderly balanced strength to the whole body's harmonious movement.

By the flexing of the throat area during the 2nd rite, I am provided with self-worthy courage to express the inner intuitive truth of my true self. Grounded on my true path and confidently guided by the UP, there is no fear of stumbling on my entrusted thoughts and wisdom that creatively resonate through a universally-hinged, resilient harmony with sound energy. Speaking clearer with integrity of budding ideas openly wakes motivational creation of inner self's reality guiding path to greatest potential attainment of united whole.

Visualizing the weakened, swollen abdomen that caused painful dysfunction of the body and the accompanying low self-esteem, the Harmony area is humbly reminded of respect for self and others when experiencing difficult situations. Getting an energy boost by successfully rehabilitating the body's disproportioned middle area has taken disciplined patience to actively reach up for divine guidance while stretching out to quietly listen during the search for answers that come in stages as each level of understanding is reached. Intuitively guided out of the dark cell of struggle and strife by taking the downs in order to enjoy the ups when higher knowledge imparts a universal remedy benefits the whole body without adverse effects and enlightens the mind and soul to quietly wait for Universal Power to intercede in matters beyond human understanding which leads to perception of self in relation to others, world, and universe. Emotionally feeling stronger with greater self-esteem, self-worth and the willpower to climb higher for myself and others with complete harmony in sight.

CHAPTER 3

<u>Love Embrace</u>

Through vital release, vibrational energy compassionately flows out real sustenance over all life supporting centers with nourishing subsistence of equality, apportioning universal empowerment for enhanced whole well-being

1. Symbol's Meaning

The symbol C illustrates how the body bends backwards from the starting kneeling position while performing the 3rd rite, named the Love Embrace, referring to the 4th energy center, which is the area of compassion and emotional balance of inner and outer worlds. The symbol signifies the letter C in compassion, cooperation, and denotes the meaning with, a positive state, such as the kneeling position that is used to show reverent love for Divine Power.

The Love Embrace, with its place in the alignment of stars as the warm glowing middle star, it is the middle rite as well as the center of all seven major energy centers. Being the center, it's like the vital root or core that unconditionally delivers universal love in deep waves throughout the inner world to readjust outer world response to changing issues.

2. Love Embrace Rite

Kneeling on a yoga-type mat for comfort and stability, elongating my spine and bringing my shoulders down to the back for a good stretch into the bent backwards position, I take a deep breath and bend backwards with my eyes closed. With rigidity felt, especially in the neck and jaw area, I opened my mouth slightly and relaxed the jaw. As life energy builds up in the heart area and spreads out, simultaneously the energy is felt gong up into the throat and then head, which is where the energy pressurizes and the visual sensation is seen as tiny high energy vibrations, like static on a visual screen. Coming back to the starting position while breathing out in the vital release phase, relaxing the spine, relieving the built-up pressure that felt like an energetic massage of my whole head, the energetic stimulation expanded to large wavy circles of lower vibrations that soothed all neuromuscular connections as it spread out like a waterfall cascading down, relaxing my whole body from deep within to the outer skin. This deep invigorating wave of massage is like a large dose of vitamin C, that was felt all the way out to the tips of the fingers and toes, causing tingling nerve sensations that helped revive the sore muscles and joints along with empathetically saturating all energy centers, and was so deeply invigorating that my body automatically swayed back and forth for a few moments. Also, pausing a little between each repetition rewards the body and mind with a cleansing stimulation during the appropriately named vital release phase.

At first, this super stimulating rite produced powerful hearing sensations, like the resonating of a huge bell's loud, long bong, as if all of the surrounding universal energy sound waves were suddenly audible. In the same way, whenever I opened my eyes during this intense moment, the color hues would turn to shades of grey and then return to normal along with the hearing as the vibrations dissipated. The extraordinary stimuli was extremely therapeutic because sharper senses and improved mental alertness became evident along with the increased health. Even though the massaging vibrations are less intense than in the beginning, they still continue to release tension in the whole body and improve the senses. Moreover, the super-sensitive, high energy vibrations may have been due to blockages in the energy centers because the sensations have decreased with daily continued practice of the rites.

Yet, another way to relieve building tension throughout the day if the practice of the rites have or haven't been done is to take a deep breath and while sitting or holding onto a firm place and bring the shoulders down and back, lifting the head up and hold for restful moment. Then letting out the breath, relax and come back to a comfortable posture, feeling the release of tension from the head down the spine as it spreads out to the extremities. Helping me to get back to clearer thinking and warmhearted helpful actions by stimulating the body's sympathetic system to humbly create balance that keeps the whole system peacefully stable even when being pushed to finish a task.

3. My Love Embrace Experience

Love for many is associated with the pain of heartache and, therefore, some will unfortunately avoid emotionally close relationships to keep from being emotionally hurt. However, the avoidance of close relationships leads many to seek shallow, short-lived relationships with the too-often shopping-around excuse that usually leaves the other in despair. As a Libra in the astrological chart, I am inwardly influenced by the heart center, desiring compassion and openness in close intimate relationships. Deeply desiring the inner heartfelt intimately close, true relationship that I have felt was meant to be ever since I was old enough to understand what a loving relationship was about, when confiding with the divine intelligence, I was assured of meeting the right one later in life, though not given specifics. Peculiarly, my intuition was able to give me a glimpse of a vision of this special person and I kept it in my mind and heart always. Extremely exhilarating as it was to happen unexpectedly when he suddenly appeared out of the blue, I was unfortunately warned that he would hurt me, but eventually he would come back to me. Fortunately, the deep heartbreak and emotional desire to have a harmonious, intimate relationship with my soul mate was the driving reason to take this well-criticized path in order to make my life right as I hold onto the hope of seeing it through. With more empathic understanding through this universal equalizing rite, I realize how important it is to have more lovingly calm stability and quiet strength in order to have compassionate understanding for others feelings, especially in close relationships.

Consoled by higher understanding that this broken-hearted search to find harmony was needed to inevitably bring me to a more intuitive awareness of the Universal Power whose true love is perpetual, enduring every kind of storm. As this comforting rite restores my basic physical and secondary emotional feelings that were critically injured from neglect and harm, created by bolstering myself like my competition to defend myself and keep false harmony, I should have allowed the universal love of empowerment to work in, through and for me. Becoming more humbly grateful, openly kind, this life transforming realm of universal energy has rebirthed my life and restored my true heart feelings. The empowering security of the Love Embrace creates a priceless like love felt from a caring parent or close family relationship, exuding stable trust that anything is possible and fixable. Being rejected and teased a lot growing up and much more in my youth helped me to earnestly seek the true pure love, intuitively felt and found solely in the deep understanding of the UP, from whom I received compassionate support and wisdom for my survival, emotions, and individual will.

The Love Embrace has also taught me how to let go of the emotional pain and fear with trust in the living energy flow of the Universal Power. A scary moment as a child helped me to use this empowering lesson as an analogy for the 2nd round of increasingly aggressive torment that came at me in a threatening way. While frightfully screaming and running away from a swarm of bees, my dad came running alongside of me and told me to stand still and then they would stop chasing me. Telling me that the bees only felt threatened and were more afraid than I, plus seeing how he was unafraid, I stood still trusting my father and closed my eyes. Feeling the profound love of the UP deeply within, surrounding me with secure empowerment and understanding that I didn't need to fear them for doing what they only innately do to survive, I learned to have empathy for those acting out in unfortunate circumstances. As the 2nd round heightened into the forewarned worse than before experience, having no secluded place to take solace and meditate quietly as in the 1st where I had the private property to walk around alone, the dreadful aggravation intensified with an acute, painful rash of sores on my head and back from the insidious events. Crying out in extreme anguish, I deeply felt their fear-stricken hostility and continued to forgive the attacks over and over, releasing the pain in exchange for the empowering love just as I had in my childhood with the bees. Then as if a virtuous vial had been broken saturating me with soothing warmth, the heartfelt universal love came bursting out with joyful delight and the horrific pain felt was transformed into energetic vibrations similar to the super-sensitive sensations first felt in the vital release phase of the Love Embrace. Transforming my tense reaction into pleas of mercy to end the assault by alleviating the aggressors' tension, the Love Embrace was powerful enough to send its stabilizing waves, calming my traumatized nerves, soothing my tense muscles, and creating assured awareness of divine security. With the empowered stabilization, divine wisdom enlightened me to how my tense dislike for their harsh, hostile actions, even though it was in defense while trying to get them off my back, only provoked them more as if to justify their attack. Now when confronted with negativity and aggression, I am equipped with empathetic understanding to flow out calming waves. Therefore, the Love Embrace with its compassionate empowerment, helps to release all tension with controlled acceptance for self and others, allowing unselfish desire for universal harmony that the UP manifests in, through and for all who make it feasible.

The Love Embrace has helped my understanding of how there are necessary moments that require bending backwards to try to work out problems and then there are distressing moments that need releasing and allowing the guidance of the higher intelligence. At times when I was described as harsh or pushy, I thought that I was helping to mend the situation, but since then I have been illuminated to when I should have released my grip and "not fight it", having learned how to better sense tension in the communication process. Being inwardly instructed to let go of the tense situation felt between my felt soulmate and I, not understanding how to act upon it and afraid of losing him if I didn't try to hold on, I now understand the importance of trusting the process rather than worrying about what is gained from it. After years of ignoring and disobeying the inner guidance when it comes to communication in relationships, I had lost divine wisdom and intuition, and therefore, it had to be regained through hard lessons. By following the intuitive guidance again, the Love Embrace has boosted my confidence to stay in a diplomatic state, allowing universal love to stabilize inner and outer tension, and stay more focused on inner peace where life energy flows unrestrained bringing inner stabilization first and then clearing the outer confusion. Conflicts disintegrate in front of me before harmful tension can get an icy grip when I am immediately made aware of a problem as universal energy builds in the heart center.

Getting inspiration from personal experiences as I write each chapter, I was working on this one as Valentine's Day came and went while deeply feeling contrite, vowing to patiently wait for my soulmate as told according to foretold message. The next day, reaffirming my deep-set trust in the hopeful message, while driving down a road where two lanes converge into one up ahead, I was suddenly alerted to car's headlights in my rear view mirror coming up on me very quickly. Knowing it was going to push its way in front of me even though I was already coming upon the convergence, I thereby allowed the rushed driver to go ahead as I have patiently learned to do. Now slowed down in stopped traffic, I was able to look at its license plate that was right in front of me and read the insightful message, "W8 4LOVE". Then I suddenly realized the powerful meaning of this epiphany at a point in the road where two lanes become one; learning to be patient at this point in my life for my orderly place, I trust that everything will flow into its rightful place as it was meant to. Enlightened with more compassionate intuition that patiently allowing the hurried car (soulmate situation) go ahead, our separate lives might converge in the future at the right point when energy is allowed to flow naturally. Suddenly coming into my view right after a friend was pushing me to try an online dating service to find a boyfriend while I recently had vowed to myself to wait for the UP to bring the right mate into my life was the first speed bump. The next speed bump came immediately after, when looking into his eyes and shockingly foretold by the higher wisdom that he was the one and then warned of trouble ahead. The third speed bump occurred like a terrible accident in slow motion when the actual heart-crushing events began to unfold once I deeply felt that he was the one.

Life energy blockages in the heart center possibly created unstable emotions, lack of compassion, and immune deficiencies which were part of the reason for my worsening health as I was unable to effectively fight off the insidious attacks, which I now know were substantially deep, and why I felt more alienated by everyone. Aware that my compassion for others as well as for myself was withered, I was weeping inside and feeling deep grief due to the lack of compassion in most of my past or present close relationships. Wanting to communicate my feelings with friends, but sensing that no one cared when I tried to reach out, I further withheld my feelings and became numb from the inside outside until I could hardly feel anything. By being out of touch with my body, my destabilized immune system was even more unable to properly detoxify the severe toxicity that built up unrestrained. Additionally, the longer that I went without feeling, the more constricted my true inner feelings became as defensive actions turned me into a hard stone that blocked the life energy flow. Detached and unable to control my emotions especially when I was being attacked whether mentally or physically, I created more tense situations because of the lack of communication on my part as well. Near the beginning of the 2nd round of chaos, I broke every rule about being patient and letting go, and instead I harshly tried to keep control as an emotionally charged situation intensified to become untouchable. The Love Embrace helped me to forgive and feel compassion instead of revenge for those who tormented me which dropped the weight that cut off the feelings of attachment and simultaneously took away the uneasiness felt when they came around as well as their tense looks. Thus, opening up to a peaceful rest and the end of all negative tension, the universal flowing love and compassion has unblocked the heart center, and therefore its deep vibrations have awakened my thoughts to a greater understanding of my feelings as well as others. Sort of like going through a revolving door, I can relate to the emotional hurt felt by others, like having my heel stepped on, then dreadfully stepping on someone else's heel accidently, it's completely understandable where they are coming from. As the Love Embrace deeply heals and sustains nerve connections with warm vibrating compassion that has brought new supple life to my corpse-like nerve branches and senses, my immunity is stronger and able to push out toxins, and my emotions are stable within normal boundaries. Genuinely alive again from the inside out and being in touch with my feelings, I am able to cry or laugh as I now feel free to communicate.

Not only has the Love Embrace opened my understanding of true compassion in order to know when to be patient and not fight the process as well as how to release the hyped up pain and fear through universal love empowerment that warmly stabilizes and gracefully balances my inner and outer worlds as the energy vibrates during the 3rd rite in the crown and brow centers, the areas of wisdom, understanding and intuition are given intelligent universal love on when and where complete release is needed for healing stabilization. Inwardly reminded of the past times that I've been in the wrong and have mistakenly caused others undeserved hurt, I've been given understanding of the wrongs that have caused me undue hurt. Now completely able to forgive others that have wounded me as I'm able to forgive myself for the wounds I've caused to others as well as to myself, I am therefore free of the harmful negative tension. As the energetic loving intelligence penetrates the damaged areas, dissolves the toxins and inflammation while the arrival of new radiant life warmly brightens all coexistence and conveys patient understanding to the cold, intolerant, hurried convergence, the soothing universal energy that inwardly calms, similarly influences my behavior to be likewise compassionate with the outside world and cooperatively share delightfully flowing attributes. Recently interacting with a hummingbird and feeling the joyful trust between us, like the fluttering felt in my heart center as it sings a delightful sound and energetically flies by to get my attention to then sit in a nearby tree to communicate back as I imitate its song is my favorite example of universal self-expressing love. Then, sharing the deep awe that fills my heart almost to the point of exploding while equally invigorating my sense of vision as I witness the beautiful always-changing, artistically painted sky above the almost equal, submissive landscape in the presence of the UP, the delightful feeling of something wonderfully new stirs inside my heart. Warmly rising to my throat and to my mind, good vibrations invigorate my inner true self to transform the new bud into its highest potential with the help of whole well-being (Health, Wealth, Love, Beauty, and Harmony).

CHAPTER 4

<u>Beauty Bud</u>

The real inner self that is creatively shaped from pure malleable thoughts rises to surface into the outside world while inwardly sustained by universal love to humbly strive for noble existence is true beauty openly expressed

1. Symbol's Meaning

The symbol ∩ is used to illustrate how the body is shaped in the table or bridge (easier alternative) position of the 4th rite, named the Beauty Bud, referring to the 5th energy center, the throat center, which is the area of self-expression and bringing forth creativity, and where to concentrate on while the life energy is felt to flow into during the this rite. The symbol signifies the letter n in the word neogenesis, which is new life that emerges out of regenerated tissue, or in the word noble, which means striving to have personal qualities of high moral principles. The symbol also somewhat resembles the natural shape from which new life emerges, such as a flower bud, cocoon, or egg that continue in regular cycles and require real sustenance in order to support life.

The Beauty Bud, whose symbol is the inverse of the Wealth Cup, takes the same kind of physical effort to receive its life energy because of the flexible strength needed to bend and lift the body in the too often stiff, weak lumbar spinal area. Just as the symbol is opposite of the Wealth Cup's, the body's movement is also opposite in direction by pushing the middle upward instead of downward which requires more control of the spine's alignment, which involves the physical areas of health, wealth, and love centers for proper support in the 4th rite movement.

2. Beauty Bud Rite

Feeling uncomfortably stiff and unattractive at first while struggling to push my swollen trunk up into the table position, I felt uneasy about being seen. While ignoring those around me, I looked upward into the abundant universal domain and concentrated on the throat center while taking a deep breath and pushed myself up off the ground. Finding it difficult to impossible in the beginning to rise up into table position, coming up part of the way or using the alternative bridge position was all I could do for a while. Despite feeling an increasing pressure in my throat, like a lump, I was deeply encouraged to focus on the higher heights that I was aiming for, which faded out the awkward physical surroundings and warm energy was felt circulating through to open my throat making it more flexible as well as my body so that the upward movement became easier and able to hold the upper position for a moment before coming back down. Sometimes, my vocal chords would vibrate out a deep sound from the energetic flow as I exhaled coming back down as they too were being toned.

After a while, I began to feel the tight areas of the body and throat loosen up as I experienced improved range of motion from more flexible joints and supple strength in the muscles so that I was able to push my body into the more difficult table position. The physical areas of health, wealth, and love along the spinal column improved with more flexible strength because of their corresponding rites as the Beauty Bud brought them altogether in a combined effort. As my body flowed up and down more easily, it was transformed into more of a graceful swan than an awkward duckling helping me to feel more relaxed and confident about being seen that resultantly relaxed my throat as the life energy freely flowed through. Now as I'm able to state my true purpose with a relaxed, confident voice, I'm also able to find solutions to problems that freeze up healthy movement, such as finding out that a nonslip yoga mat is my preferred surface for this and all of the other rites, except the first rite that requires free movement, because it keeps the hand and foot placement secure for stable movement and makes activation of the inner core easier without slipping or stopping to reposition.

3. My Beauty Bud Experience

Tonight, being one of many now, as I finish the rites and look up at the stars, I feel younger and can remember back to the awesome powerful feeling of looking up into the country sky full of stars imagining that their energy was transforming me into a universally natural, beautiful girl as a tormented youth. After my classmates began taking advantage of my shyness and thin stature, the situation escalated when I tried to cover up what seemed to be acne with a useless treatment cream and it worsened into a horrible parasitic attack on my upper body. So, after being teased constantly about my physical characteristics leading up to a tense argument that ended with a swollen nose after being punched in the face, turning away from the horrific state of affairs, I released my fight of being accepted as I collapsed on my bed openly crying out to the divine intelligence. Feeling the intensity of energy in my throat area after sobbing for a while also supported my inner real self-expression as communication with the UP became an uplifting experience, like a trusted good friend.

Going for long nurturing walks on my parents' secluded property after school became intuitively beneficial as I was rewarded with peaceful meditation sensing the powerful life energy of the vibrant natural surroundings stabilize my inner being. Meditating on the noble life that I was striving for, I earnestly continued my spirit-lifting tours around the woods and huge, protective oak trees while gratefully maintaining the beautiful array of life found on the rich grounds that felt as if they were deeply nurturing me and the escalating drama faded away. Absorbed in the natural beauty unfolding around me and the increasingly real self-visualization that was inwardly assured of being fulfilled, I felt an excitement of new life stirring within as I began to physically notice increased energy almost every day. Mesmerized and thankful as I reverently self-expressed internal gratitude and trustful requests to the UP, I climbed to breathtaking heights that further transformed my whole well-being as I noticed more vibrant eye color in the irises and thicker, new hair that filled in the thin spots that were caused by the parasitic sores. Confidently focused on the new life that was emerging, gradually the inner vision of my real self radiantly materialized into a creation of beauty and strength of both mind and body as I continued to soar to higher accomplishments with upright efforts, such as being an honors student in high school and college.

Just before the 2nd round heated up, feeling confident about my muscular body after winning 1st place in heavyweight, novice and masters divisions, I received many compliments as I rollerbladed down the beach strand. However, inwardly feeling too muscular and bulky, especially when the inflammation began creeping in and the abdomen was starting to swell, I was pushed away by my heartfelt mate when I went to kiss him after having some drinks with him and friends. Many months later, being told by him that I didn't have the right characteristics without any explanation of what it meant, I felt terribly less acceptable and unable to express my concern.

Blindly, I figured that my nose was the problem after he had mentioned how he loved my eyes and my body but had only really kissed me a couple of times near the beginning of the relationship. Adding to the confusion shortly after this crushing episode, a female acquaintance told me that I needed to look more feminine, and then, within a couple months, two distinct females that weren't related to each other in any way advised me that changing my nose would help me look more attractive. Beginning to recall how past close relationships had played out the same way with minimum kissing and the many past insults received, I became obsessed about my distorted face and began to believe outside advice. Looking at my face in photos, disbelieving the better pictures thinking that it was the camera's angle that created a mirage of beauty, I started believing the reflection in the mirror was correctly showing my disproportionate prominent feature instead of focusing on the real inner being connection that had become inflexibly brittle and fractured due to many years of neglecting the inner voice and instead selfishly seeking my prideful ways.

Desiring the approval of my soulmate and friends, I went to a trusted plastic surgeon and discussed how I felt my nose was out of proportion to my face and my concern that worsening body inflammation might be causing the unbecoming facial feature that seemed to be creating tense reactions towards me by others. The doctor didn't think that the inflammation was a problem, brushing it aside probably because it wasn't his area of expertise, but warned me that complete satisfactory results from nose alterations were difficult. Given photos taken with sketches over my nose area, I quickly half-heartedly approved of the procedure after telling me that he didn't take requests for making noses look like someone else. Deciding on a surgery date and inwardly getting a warning that my soulmate wouldn't like the nose change, I continued to ask for more guidance that never came. After getting the same kind of indifferent responses that I did about my health problems when mentioned my pending nose alteration to anyone, I painfully shrugged it all off as well as the notion of directly asking my soulmate if there was something wrong with my face. Instead I hoped that the change would make me look and feel better, ending tense reactions and open my airway to breathe better during intense workouts, plus stop an audible whistle heard when breathing deeper.

Oblivious at the time or not wanting to face up to the real truth that I still had not released the soulmate problem as inwardly instructed when I first met him, not realizing that being told to be patient meant not acting on my part to try to fix things, I let my tense feelings create a cork of confusion and insecurity that made it even more difficult to just open up and communicate my real emotions spoken and unspoken. Months later, my irrational decision with permanent consequences became drastically more evident when I went to see my heartfelt mate at his request with the worst timing as my top layer of facial skin was beginning to peel from a recent deep-layer facial recommended by the same doctor that performed the ill-prepared rhinoplasty.

Given quiet uneasy looks as I walked up to him made me immediately tense up around him and even more so when I asked him what he meant a year ago when asking me about being intimate with his friend to which a cold remark came out. Wondering why he had asked me to come over to his place, I nervously blocked out the inner prompting to explain that I was going through a very confusing health issue that was distorting my physical body and misfortunately had rhinoplasty with the hope of making my face more attractive after the time that he had pushed me away. Handing me a glass of ice cold water after asking if I wanted a drink, I sat on a couch shivering while he sat quietly opposite of me across the room telling me to put the throw lying over the couch on me if I was cold. Unable to say anything that I wanted to except that I didn't need the blanket and was fine, which was a complete cover-up, he then told me that he was going to have a monogamous relationship that I certainly understood didn't involve me. Trying to make a joke such as asking for a rain check wouldn't even come out, as I sat horrifically frozen and speechless because of the icy tension in the deadly quiet room feeling helpless as I saw my current life at that very moment take a nose dive into a death spiral. Finally after a long uncomfortable silence, he told me that he had things to do, and after walking me to the door and giving me a very weak hug, he said that he liked me the way that I was before as I walked out the door. Sadly recalling that regretful moment that I was rolled into the operation room and suddenly sensing a severe warning to call off the surgery, but in a somewhat state of shock from this instantaneous command, I didn't have a chance to get a word out probably because the doctor saw my apprehension and had the anesthesiologist immediately put me under.

Hoping for the best as the inflammation decreased, the airway also decreased in diameter making it harder to breathe than before as my nasal passage would close when deeply breathing while running or intensely working out. Due to the bridge of my nose being broken as a part of the rhinoplasty, it was like breathing through tiny cocktail-straw holes and almost completely closed when congested. Told that the constriction would lessen after the inflammation ceased never happened and an in-office procedure to lessen the tightness at the tip of the nose didn't alleviate the uncomfortable feeling either. Four years later, still numb and closed up as I grew more uneasy about my facial characteristics evolving further away from my real inner self-identity, I determinedly sought a professional referral that apprehensively led me to a reputable nose doctor, nicknamed the nose doctor, who said that he wouldn't be able to help me with my clown nose, but he would be able to give me the nose that I wanted if I brought in a picture of someone else's nose that similar to what I wanted. Even though inwardly warned of the possible problems and the additional financial hardship that the second surgery would bring, I was more unable to live with the tight, unflattering nose even after being told by the doctor that widening the nose bridge back to the original structure couldn't be done, which meant not getting closer to the prior real self-image. Going to the follow-up appointment after the surgery, I was devastated when told that my end cartilage, that gives the nose tip its shape, had been removed and the nostrils tucked in, which made the tip and the nostril openings smaller. Although specifically requesting that my main concern was to breathe easier, I would wake up desperately gasping for air as the surgery created more inflammation than before, and to add to the painful chaotic recovery, I had to go into the doctor's office regularly for painful injections of filler to even out the sunken areas that according to the doctor would be indefinite. Without my knowledge, I had already paid for years of these visits for the unwanted filler as it was included in the double the price of the first rhinoplasty.

The Five Rites came to my rescue in perfect timing as my health was at its worst ever experienced, with an awkward looking, unattractive abdomen accompanied by painful body inflammation, and my head with an inflamed, unstructured nose that looked worse than the swollen nose of my troubled youth along with the horrible rash of sores on my head and upper back. As the 2nd round of harassments heated up, first felt at the workplace and first seen at the gym where I started practicing the rites, the improvement of life energy flowing into my throat area abundantly quickened the real inner self to begin its restorative process. However, just like in nature, when creation has been destroyed by a disaster, the gloom of darkness takes time to fade, and the deeper the destruction the longer the damage persists. Therefore, even when the awful painful condition didn't improve or even worsened, I persevered by focusing on the envisioned goal that was universally sustained by the life energy of the energy centers giving me the confident promise of natural beauty developing out of the real inner self. By keeping in mind that the infrastructure of a building is more important for confident stability and strength than the attractive decorated façade; being more flexibly aware than an inanimate object, my façade is more naturally equipped to be restored from within by the inner connection to the true source of the infrastructure of the inner whole well-being.

The Beauty Bud, not only improves my flexibility and strength for graceful movements as it pushes out tension in the body by bending outward in the table or bridge position, but it also improves communication by unblocking the throat area with its energetic flow of creativity from the UP so that true sound of real self-expressive thoughts effortlessly flow radiantly deep into the universe. The most critical time is when the newly transforming life begins to bud, like a sprout from out of the ground, and must continually release its grip on useless limitations to fully flourish and openly express its real inner desire of creative beauty. By raising my true inner expression up to the highest heights while focusing on the inner real self that is restoratively created, humbly respecting the UP's abundant life energy and restorative wisdom, I freely allowed the intuit truth of higher wisdom to flow through my inner voice to communicate the remedy to my uniquely caused health problems while dropping the weighted trauma. Intuitively finding appropriate treatments that were natural and without side-effects, as creative ideas flowed in while being guided to where and what I was to research, benefited me more than all of the doctors' visits combined due to their lack of knowledge of what I was going through and/or didn't want to help, which lowered my morale only momentarily. Besides uplifting my mental state, the intelligent nature of the unconventional medicine went to other hidden areas of need to manifest better health inside out as I slowly began to feel and see improvements such as more youthful definition in the face and body and new healthy hair replacing the coarse white hair that had fallen out.

First of all, by disregarding the outside withering structures, a deeper real inner connection was created resulting in a clearer communication of the inner visualization that was richly opened up to its visible goal instructing the order in which to push forward as the inner connection to the UP kept my progress on a successful passage veering around or through the difficult surroundings. Secondly, by believing that this inner connection was greater than existence itself, the real inner self in its wake grew more resilient and brilliant in the Beauty Bud rite, in which it energetically materialized as a tighter defined abdomen and slender musculature. Thirdly, as true purpose desires richer existence, rising above the painfully encroaching drama below, greater heights are aimed for and whole being radiantly emerges, powerfully transformed, courageously souring straight to illuminated success. Finally, the Beauty Bud's creative motivation being similar to the Wealth Cup's disciplined desire, has encouraged me to push in noble efforts for real goals, which pays off in balanced energetic movements, graceful characteristics and gracious qualities for highest possible achievement. Now, as the true inner-perceived image once again vigorously materializes from the mound of chronic, toxic inflammation and pitifully frozen façade, I am drawn appreciably closer in reverent adoration to the UP, whose deep meaningful message that had come to, for, and through me, especially because of the outside stranglehold of aggravation. Communicating through universal love with stable emotions, I am secure with expressing my inner thoughts created by disciplined guidance and feel comfortable in my flexibly transformed image.

Furthermore, when I go deeper into my sustaining roots of pure universal compassion to greatly endure lengthy adversarial hardships, the more fascinatingly luminous the regal beauty shines within as richer springs are ventured and moving ideas are formed. The real intriguing display of life that distinctively flows out entertains the alert senses with awe-striking qualities like a masterpiece that engages the mind in a state of wonder. On the contrary, attention to the superficial hard shell, particularly when imitatively constructed, like outside withering structures that fall apart when inflexible to a change in direction by sudden force, constricts and disrupts the true flow of the inner being preventing its potential universal contribution for purposeful success. Whereas, authentic existence is inherently fragile requiring consistent maintenance by the unlimited power of the inner connection, which requires the real inner self to maintain a consistent relationship with in order to thrive through cold fronts, dangerous currents, and intrusive assaults that inevitably try to steal away its life energy. With spring almost here, I am once again focusing on the emerging nature, captivated by the vividly rich color hues that enhance each other as I feel the unified energy pour out enriching my well-being of self-expression to flow resonantly. Attentively encouraging meditation on the inner real creation, like before in my youth during the cold, disparaging, confusing storm, my body and mind stretches out and transforms in more versatile ways, my self-confidence is attentively boosted to boldly express the real radiated self that is more accommodating than the stiff outer conflict that undermines and inconsiderately wastes vital energy.

Wishing to transfer outwardly radiating relaxed waves that have soothingly massaged my awkward, uncomfortable façade transforming it into real brilliant beauty that easily translates my welcoming life purpose so that I no longer detract from the universal-loving self-expression, my desire is to relax the outside tension gently coaxing their icy grip to release and open up to the life flow. When the vulnerable side is exposed, the most striking colors and textures are experienced, therefore, in the Beauty Bud, they become the strongest and vibrant when the highest potential effort is made to push them out into the outside surroundings. With renewed willpower to encourage new life, give it loving care that the UP provides through the inner connection, and daily celebrate its arrival and growth by believing in the inner source of creation, my undesirable, destructed, useless nose was restructured by daily intelligent guidance as to how to, when to, and what to do in order to have a healthy functioning feature of compassionate expression for complete harmony. Most important is this inner connection to the UP that illuminates to push forward in pure, upward directions for flexible transformation of the whole being resulting in real inner contentment.

Therefore, by stating my vision of pushing the limit to serve as many families as possible by giving them a thoroughly clean, desirable home to come back to after working so hard for their domestic accommodations so that someday I might have my own created solitude, I continued to push myself to my highest potential while keeping focused on the real inner self connection to abundant life and ultimately catalyzed the imagined creation. In addition, learning to openly express my emotions with calmingly warm confidence from the stabilizing universal love that flexibility softens and transforms my whole being into compassionate open arms, I continue to strive for higher accomplishments in this life here on this planet in this expansive energetic universe.

Life energy blockages in the throat center possibly contributed to the repression of thoughts after becoming more inflexible in communicating my inner feelings because of grief in the heart center from the lack of compassion by others, which in turn possibly caused a hypo-thyroid problem after experiencing signs of inflammation along with physical and mental fatigue. Understanding now that when I tensed up from stressing over a situation, my throat also tensed up making my voice stiffly harsh along with my words and body movements, which complicated the whole communication flow creating a domino effect. The confidence built by self-expression in the 4th rite has helped to create positive experiences for the good that satisfy my heart so that others' lack of compassion doesn't bring me down anymore and grief is immediately swept away with gratifying universal life energy. Instead, this tough time of not being fairly treated is manifesting more imagination and creativeness to reach higher heights of the limitless energetic knowledge of the UP, who warmly guides my inner thoughts while patiently understanding my awkward existence, so that I might break through the finite barrier of communication between this world and the celestial. This cannot happen unless I maintain my humble course expressly permitting the UP's energy to be my strong support and vocal guidance. All tension now results in a faster heart rate activating the heart center flowing compassion to the problem, soothing the whole body and mind, sending warm waves of the comforting inner voice echoing gently, guiding intuitive thoughts opening wider to higher wisdom, creating healing actions and emotions for highest possible will for all.

CHAPTER 5

<u>Harmony Swing</u>

Forever fluidly flowing stronger, grounded in stable, reinforced foundation, the bud creatively enjoys versatile universal harmony while accordingly expressing its real self out into the world using its highest potential to soar to greater heights with empowered attributes of an orderly synergistic system

1. Symbol's Meaning

The symbol **O** is used to illustrate the combined positions of the body as it flexes back and forth in the 5th rite, accordingly named the Harmony Swing, and refers to the 6th and 7th energy centers, which includes the brow center, the area of visualization, intuition and logic, and the crown center, the area of thought and spiritual connection to the highest power, respectively. The life energy seems to illuminate these centers located at the brow and crown of the head as the energy centers along the spine alternate back and forth from highest to lowest points like riding on a teeter totter in this rite. Illumination from the insightful connection to the highest level of universal wisdom, the inner being is logically challenged to be proactive and attain ultimately desired optimum achievement.

The Five Rites came to my rescue in perfect timing as my health was at its worst ever experienced, with an awkward looking, unattractive abdomen accompanied by disfiguring inflammation, and my head with an inflamed, unstructured nose that looked worse than the swollen nose of my troubled youth along with the horrible rash of sores on my head and upper back. As the 2nd round of harassments heated up, first at the workplace and then at the gym where I started practicing the rites, the improvement of life energy flowing into my throat area abundantly quickened the real inner self to begin its restorative process. However, just like in nature, when creation has been destroyed by a disaster, the gloom of darkness takes time to fade, and the deeper the destruction the longer the damage persists. Therefore, even when the awful painful condition didn't improve and even worsened in some areas, I persevered by focusing on the envisioned goal that was universally sustained by the life energy of the energy centers giving me the confident promise of natural beauty developing out of the real inner self. By keeping in mind that the infrastructure of a building is more important for confident stability and strength than the attractive decorated façade; inwardly being more flexibly aware through the universal flow of energy, my façade is more naturally equipped to be restored from within by the inner connection to the true source of the infrastructure of the inner whole well-being than through outside cosmetic surgery.

The symbol signifies the letter O in organization of the combined areas of thoughtful spiritual wisdom and intuitive visualization that unifies all energy centers in better synchronization fortifying the physical and spiritual inner being and offering real-timely helpful guidance so that more useful assets can be added in a secure, solid way every day to thereby fulfill the living purpose that is most bountiful regarding the combined whole existence of a being and the surrounding communities.

The wonderful symmetry of the O's in the Harmony Swing production of whole well-being is how these energy center ends that are opposite in their functions but similar in their outward symbols come together in harmonious balance. Health is the inner basic need while Harmony is the outer shared need, yet both are similar in being a circle, which is a strong unit on its own but requires the other in order to completely function as a successful congruent, just like opposing cells of the body need each other. Furthermore, both circles have inner circles that enhance the unit's existence but are not openly acknowledged. Health's stability is enriched with creativity as well as pleasurable emotions in intimate relationships and social interaction, while Harmony's balance with thought and omnipotent power is broadened by intuitive visualization of the inner realm self and others in order to give logical guidance for successful purpose. Illustrating the Harmony Swing, the left side or foundation with its basic survival instincts involving physical stability and creative pleasurable experiences, essentially needs the right side or mental lattice of intuition, visualization and inner realm connection if an everlasting network of expansive growth is desired.

2. Harmony Swing Rite

At first when getting into the starting position on hands and flexed toes, I felt weak and tight in the joints and muscles, especially in the shoulders and neck, while flexing upward, and then uncomfortable pressure was felt in the head and chest as well when bringing my head down to the lower position as my hips were raised to the higher position of the second half of the rite. Although a weak, tight, imbalanced body slowed down the otherwise fluid motion of swaying the body up and down, created difficulty standing back up along with lightheadedness afterwards. Patiently working through the difficulties while slowly swaying up and down, the toning effect of the life energy flowing through lubricated the tight joints and toned the muscles lessening all the uneasiness.

Finally, the 5th rite's flowing movement became light and airy instead of burdensome and constricted at the same time that intuition, understanding and wisdom improved bringing harmony to the whole situation with clear perception to lighten up the bleak condition.

Similar to the Health Spin in its lively movement, but being the opposite bookend of the rites, the Harmony Swing is more like a thrilling cool-down ride on a swing that distributes the life energy in an organized manner while the perceptive reasoning area is aroused. When the stagnant areas were opened up to equalizing flow, my body was more stably balanced to swing up and down in a smooth rhythmic movement, resulting in faster motion that improved my coordination as the improved muscles and joints efficiently worked in balanced cooperation. With improved synchronization of all necessary areas, the dynamic movement increased as the stronger core and abdominal muscles synergistically interacted to pump the momentum. Cheerfully clearing my mind and flexing my spine, like an hourglass filled with fluidly flowing universal energy, my whole body is revived with every refreshing wave like riding on a teeter-totter or swing.

3. My Harmony Swing Experience

Due to energy blockages in the brow and crown area that caused cloudy understanding and weakened intuition due to not following inner spiritual guidance for a long time, I was confused as to what to do after many failed attempts at finding a rightful harmonious purpose and where I belonged in the world, thus bad decisions compounded future actions by unclear perceived guidance. Also, mental problems, such as psychosis and obsession sunk in causing self-doubt and low self-esteem, which explains why I allowed the outside world to wrongly influence how I felt about my body characteristics, such as my nose. Once I began performing the Five Rites, I once again regained the insightful spiritual intelligence that I had before the years of selfishly searching for my purpose while slowly disconnecting from the UP. With more insightful wisdom as I continue to look up for guidance in this 5th rite, clarity of intuitive understanding revealed that toxins placed on my scalp by uncooperative coworkers were the reason for my body's inflammation, facial distortion, and emotional misery.

Continued practice of the rites began to clear away the health problems as the 5th rite, with its restorative flow, lifted and swept away the body's discomfort and pressure along with the lightheadedness, and resultantly returned insightful understanding allowing spiritual intelligent guidance to good decisions. Equally rewarded with healthy emotions, such as optimism and lightheartedness, brighter moments illuminated the darkness to shine on golden opportunities to give way to more healing of health problems that took constant effort to trust was the right path to success. After learning to follow sound guidance, being inwardly informed of the importance of herbs, hot spices, and essential oils was the turning point to seeing better health after several trips to different doctors emptied my hope and pocketbook, successful insightful searching turned up natural healing recipes that gradually, but definitely remedied the deep-seated destruction. Having constant aggravation to my health from continued insidious intrusion, attentive intuition to follow intelligent guidance ultimately led to finding quality essential oils from a company that uses responsible sourcing, which is the process of selecting the correct plant source and knowledgeable growers that harvest the essential oils while fairly supporting their harvesting business. Therefore, it gave me deep satisfaction in buying pure essential oils that had powerful healing qualities as well as supporting a good cause around the world, in addition to clearing out of deep toxins, improving my body's health from inside out as well as soothing my emotions. Finally, true guidance has imparted a confidence in the ability to heal most health problems as the basic health area is grounded and lighter with issues relieved so that I am no longer negatively affected by useless visits to doctors that are ill-equipped.

Relationally being intuitive as a preschooler, I distantly watched my classmates nervously bolstered themselves in their noticeably unbecoming facades trying to make it seem as if they were more important than their competition. Growing more confident in my real self-image by drawing close to the UP due to the unfriendliness of many who I met usually through their self-centered pushy arguments, I desired not to be forceful or unkind like the bullish players that push others down in order to stay at the top while leaving others emotionally numb, critically wounded, or walking wounded, including themselves, the outwardly victorious ones at the top. Therefore, I solely learned to enjoy the peacefully inviting, loving warmth of nature's pure energetic life until someone with the same desires came along and did, which became my first real friend relationship. Allowing the understanding and spiritual wisdom in to guide my life, I constantly experienced empowerment over conflicts by standing still in quiet strength.

In the same way as the tormented youth, I passively watched how the 1st round of harassing attacks reached a horrendous climax, realizing that they were played out in the same aggressive way as the elementary school years. It was when I let go of the struggle of wanting to be harmoniously part of the student activities, released the tension, and passively allowed spiritual wisdom and understanding to flow in, stabilizing my body and clearing my mind of confusion that it was clarified to me that they were acting in fear like the swarm of bees. In addition, I was made aware that they were also deeply jealous of me as a good student and athlete in gym classes remembering that I always received high grades and physically excelled past most of them in sports, and therefore, was teased about being so smart as well as skinny on many separate occasions by different classmates. By allowing in the empowering understanding and creative insight, I overlooked their unkind, childish behavior, and then, no longer traumatized, quietly delighted in the empowerment as the frustrated attempts of intimidation mounted up. With spiritual intelligence, I saw unlimited possibilities that opened up a broader, meaningful, higher existence than the immediate suffocation of current habitation. However, later on after moving away from the strife, hurriedly venturing ahead of inner guidance, I was subtly charmed by the tranquil beguiling side, letting down my inner guard, I became confusingly incapacitated and unable to break free of negative energy relationships. Through the 5th rite, I clearly understand that the inner connection to the UP is more real and sustaining than superficial connections of prideful destruction as I once again desire not to be unkind.

In an interesting way, the Harmony Swing with its up and down movement has encouraged my wealth area of understanding to see that basic survival requires a disciplined cordialness in workplace relationships and that a quiet strength is necessary when taking any criticism even if it isn't deserved for complete success and harmony. Then, universal wisdom incited that it was my monetary responsibility to give back or give up in the personal effort for universal equality in order to build stable relationships that satisfy each other's individual willpower for unified success. Therefore, the clarity of giving more than received was highly understood as putting more effort into a project than compensated for was later recognized through better opportunities to come and higher standings along with improved self-control, self-esteem, and so on, of which exuded confidence resulting in more respectful cooperation. So as a result, greater success is accomplished on the highest potential path and by heeding insightful advice to avoid appealingly easier paths that lead down deceptive alleys of wasted time and resources as well as the loss of respect.

Lovingly in the heart area, as the chest waves up and down in the movement of this rite, I feel as if I am flying through the sky as it equalizes the pressure in all energy centers easing compassionate accord through insightful efforts of understanding to harmonize my inner and outer concerns. Freely forgiving myself and others of oppression by soaring to higher impulses of consciousness that reflect wisdom and guidance of all life energy in universal union of acceptance, insight into the fragility of this homeostatic earthly life supplies my compassion with all the more understanding to cherish the time here with heartfelt relationships. Finally given peace from the heartache of the absence of the long-awaited soulmate relationship, my heart center has opened up to a more universal love for all that includes the ones who have caused pain and misery, for now I have spiritual understanding that is beyond this world's comprehension of love, for which there is no words.

With improved flexibility, the throat center is open to true voice of inner self-expression as I find the real inner self again while enjoying my special place in nature and its wildlife that put their trust in us as I now insightfully understand. While my life is being steadfastly rebuilt, my agile intuition and higher understanding discloses how the buffeting caused harmful rigidity that stunted my contribution to the outside world, and thereby has opened up communication and accountability of my actions so that complete focus on the whole picture of my highs and lows in life are now responsibly logical. Additionally, as my creativity is being flexed open more ideas will rise to the surface while the willpower confidently motivates the thoughts intuitively enlightened.

The Harmony Swing giving intelligent guidance to all energy centers that the basic requirements of each area's maneuverability demands the intuitive guidance of the higher intelligence, which bestows the understanding that every given part, even the highest, must be flexible enough to communicate its needs or concerns, and at least, understand the capacity to have empathy for the other connected parts in order for the whole unit to possess the organizational qualities of harmony. Accordingly, I do feel and show empathy for the inflexible crowd that will break under their own pressure as the criticizing gossipers will not be able to go through the intensity of abuse that I did while being forced to a low standing, which is evident as their building self-friction encroaches. In other words, each position currently held, whether high or low in ranking, needs to adaptably bend with the turbulent storms and take the its downward turn in order for the orderly evolving cycle to eventually spring the yielding position up to a higher, deserved place. As a result, the whole is richly sustained with inner strength to equally benefit all positions so that the collective condition is stable and not weighted more on one side causing destructive imbalance.

Finally, with tolerance, I fervently enjoy the downward enriching ride as I gain strength from insightful universal wisdom that brings health, wealth, love, beauty and harmony synergistically together with calming effects. My improved spiritual intelligence and understanding is better utilized through a quickened awareness and creative imagination to bring about harmony with the outside world, asserting improvement at each hurdle for increased accord with others, to live a more highly productive life that defeats tyranny through synergized organization of all areas. Wonderfully finding my way again with the UP's support, the Five Rites have proactively re-established inner strength of empowerment and overall guidance to all the main areas of life.

CHAPTER 6

<u>Whole Well-being</u>

O   U   C   ∩   O

HEALTH   WEALTH   LOVE   BEAUTY   HARMONY

The melody of the symbols as they imitate the natural cycles of life, lunar phases, ocean waves is only the surface, for there is a complex intricate network of meaningful tones in their melodious rhythm and rhyme as the mysterious depth is explored

1. Comparative natural examples

The flow of whole well-being balance, like an ocean wave that is created by the welling up of water, the Health Spin, rising to a crest, the Wealth Cup, which bends over releasing built-up pressure, the Love Embrace, to push onward, the Beauty Bud, towards its intended purposeful direction with strong organization, the Harmony Swing, and then the cycle repeats.

Creation of new life is another example with the Health Spin which is stirred into action, like a seed or fertilized egg, then the Wealth Cup, which is connected to its desired individual will increases with disciplined effort, as the Love Embrace, which gives compassion to cooperatively turn and equalize its love for the surrounding world, with the Beauty

Bud, which nobly pushes out the real inner self to flexibly self-express with trust, and the Harmony Swing, which through strongly organized, ever-growing intuitive wisdom bends and bows in rhythmic obedience while creatively bridging the individual's customary gap between the soul and the Universal Power.

2. Universal Orderly Balance

The overall name of the orderly balanced method came about when expressly sounding out the first letter of each symbols' meanings, Health, Wealth, Love, Beauty, and Harmony that were surprisingly revealed one day when singing a cheerful melody of gratefulness to the UP for the wonderful rites that were unexpectedly presented to me and restoring my mind and body to a more youthful state, in which resulted, "WHOLE WELL-BEING."

In order for the body and mind to be at its best potential for a good life with whole well-being, the energy centers need to be maintained regularly, just like the whole body needs regular cleansing. The important function of the heart center in whole well-being is explained with the above horizontal illustration of the energy centers, with the heart area being the balancing point, also called the fulcrum, pivot, or heart, which is where the triangle is pointed at, and the head being on the right side. With the help of the middle rite, named the Love Embrace, the energetic empathic connection flows out to all areas to join them in a resonating choir of universal acceptance through its massaging vibrations that dissolve the gradual, rigid complacency. Opening the flow of life energy between all the areas increases the circulation of life energy through the body as the energy centers are freely spinning in synchronous organization, which creates whole well-being. Therefore, the Love Embrace as the pivotal heart keeps both sides in cooperatively caring equilibrium by constantly sending out compassionate universal love to wherever tension resides.

Then, when life suddenly becomes a heap of trouble with all kinds of stress from every direction leaving the harmony area in disharmony by keeping thoughtful guidance off course, the heart center will strongly deliver awakening high energy signals to the sunken right side of the life board, illustrated above, to alert and assist critical thinking for carrying out the best possible steps for getting back on the clearest course. By sending down radiant waves of universal warmth, the heart center also dissolves the frigidness in order to restart a healthy production of willpower for survival created through inner thoughts by sharing potential actions that avert a major disaster. Similarly on the other end of the plank, when the unequally heavy, physically needy side of health and wealth is too busy searching for basic needs, a compassionate balance is found as the stimulating massage of the heart center stabilizes the neuromuscular connections and soothes the heavy emotions, thereby energetically lightening up the left side of the life board to reasonably see the higher intelligent benefit of a harmonious relationship with the real inner being in order to reach true life creativeness and the higher understanding of all so that goals are attainable.

As shown below in order of the rites' symbols, from the top area of the Harmony Swing to the bottom area of the Health Spin, as they are stacked when standing upright, the Wealth Cup and Beauty Bud, the 2nd and 4th areas respectively, open up towards the 3rd area of the Love Embrace, which being the heart area is also physically the main artery that sends out waves of stabilizing support and needed supple sustenance. Therefore, the Wealth Cup opens up to the Love Embrace for more agile power in order to sustain confident fulfillment of its highest potential and to bring the other energy centers in alliance for unified good will. With empowered motivation, the Wealth Cup gives more worthy effort to the Health Cup's stable circulation, and thus bringing greater equilibrium to the inner and outer being. Reciprocating, the Wealth Cup gives the Love Embrace greater willpower to overcome all negativity and to put forth a continual effort to distribute universal acceptance to all. Similarly, the Beauty Bud opens to the Love Embrace for real sound expression of inner emotion from true inner reflection and therefore, openly transmits true meaning through all energy centers while patiently enduring as the stiff areas resolve their inflexibility. As the throat center is gently manipulated, the articulation of creative thoughts through inner compassion resounds upward and throughout. In turn, the Harmony Swing's unlimited communication establishes intuitively intelligent caring consideration in core stability with higher discipline for unified willpower fairly expressed to show flexibility for shared harmonious existence at the highest potential of compassionate life for large and small, near and far, in this powerfully connected universe.

V.   O   STRENGTH

Synergistic strength from the insightful organization of all energy centers: I.) Health Spin circulation, II.) Wealth Cup neuromuscular connections, III.) Love Embrace equilibrium, IV.) Beauty Bud flexibility, and V.) Harmony Swing universal guiding strength. (*A distributing fan to oscillate together for increased production of synergistic circulation as well as an exhilaratingly wrap up of the exercises with focus on the brow and crown energy centers*)

IV.   ∩   FLEXIBILITY

The self-expression of natural beauty is articulately communicated with true efforts to bring out inner thoughts that transform the inner sustained being to flexibly radiate real life.

(Deeply working the joints to increase the elasticity of the body and mind with focus on the throat energy center)

III.   C   EQUILIBRIUM

Through complete release, the relaxing vital flow compassionately renews and sustains from inside out, and thereby imparts empowerment for complete equilibrium that will bring strong illuminated rewards. (*Extending the spine and deep stimulation of neuromuscular connections with focus on the heart energy center*)

II.   U   CONNECTION

The union of neuromuscular-connected parts in disciplined effort continue to reach up to Universal Power and stretch out to fan the fire of individual will that satisfies the true inner desire. (*Warmly stimulating the inner core and stabilizing muscles while flexing the neck for stronger support with focus on the solar plexus energy center, the middle abdomen*)

I.   O   CIRCULATION

Origin of life must be stirred and warmed so that healthy circulation reaches all vital areas. (*Activates life energy, stirring up all areas with focus on the root and sacral energy centers*)

3. Quintessential example of whole well-being

With a strong bond, like the diamond that can withstand surrounding pressure, the whole well-being is fortified through the Five Rites by sharing the benefits of the life energy flow that creates a universally balanced environment inside and out. Increased pressure is balanced out with the help of the heart center that flows equalizing vibrations to all connections. Deeply intrigued by how each rites' related energy center is activated to improve life energy flow and the corresponding body functions, and more amazed by how each center responds to the others' need in a mutual effort to restore harmonious balance for whole well-being. Humbly with patience and a closely abiding bond with the Universal Power, I continue to strive for harmony in and around me in this multi-vacillated world. Therefore, as the universal life energy flows through this multi-faceted bond, the universal strength of the Wealth Cup's individual will is the flame that keeps the Health Cup's physical needs circulating in the right direction while the Love Embrace and Beauty Bud, like compassionate wings in true flight, give reinforcing support to reach the highest point as the Harmony Swing's ever-increasing intuitive help gets directions from the UP's boundless realm of wisdom.

Although it takes time to see adversity turn around, just like a turning wheel's momentum takes time to stop and then start turning in the opposite direction, it's the time in between changing directions that seems to last forever. Many times, conditions become worse as friction heats up when there is an effort to stop a current action or desire, because the immediate rigid environment is resistant to change and is incompatible due to the surrounding's uncertainty of the change even when it is for the good. However, by continued effort to press on for the overall good, the disassembled life clinging on to the thin, unraveled connection to the UP is able to rebuild a strong tie again. Therefore, my desire to heal my fractured life has come about so that I would release my self-defeating attempts and come back up in a powerful universal way that would instructively lead many others to heal up their scattered live as well. Already sensitized to this inner connection to universal power because of my past experience in healing from traumatizing events, I sense that my all-entombing trouble was not for my death as many have thought or wished it to be, but for the Universal Power's beneficial purpose to be brilliantly shown.

With a strong bond, like the diamond that can withstand surrounding pressure, the whole well-being is fortified through the Five Rites by sharing the benefits of the life energy flow that creates a universally balanced environment inside and out. Increased pressure is balanced out with the help of the heart center that flows equalizing vibrations to all connections. Greatly intrigued by each of the five rites' universal life flow into each energy center improving the corresponding body functions of each activated center, I am also amazed by how each center responds to the others in a mutual effort to restore harmonious balance for whole well-being. With patience and a closely abiding bond with the Universal Power, I continue to strive for harmony around me in this multi-vacillated world. Therefore, as the universal life energy flows through this multi-faceted bond, the power of the Wealth Cup's individual will is the flame that keeps the Health Cup's physical needs circulating in the right direction while the Love Embrace and Beauty Bud, like wings in flight, give reinforcing strength to reach the highest potential of the Harmony Swing's ever-increasing intuitive relationship with the UP's boundless wisdom.

Rather than fighting the friction of those resistant to progress during the time of changing directions like I did at first refusing to understand the whole balance, which only complicated the downward ride making it last longer and more difficult to stop, I positively relaxed letting the chaos lower me with hair-raising momentum in order for the universal life energy, in which I fully trusted, to rebound me with energetic stimulus. With the Five Rites activating the UP's life energy to rightly build my life again, I am empowered to conscientiously become more flexibly connected in my self-expression, more equally stable in my love for the outside world, more confident in my intended personal power, and more eagerly motivated to circulate for good relationships and health. Therefore, the inescapable antagonist was imposingly necessary to strengthen the agonist of ecstasy.

Being forever thankful for my closer walk with the Universal Power, the UP, the struggle to find whole well-being has been more rewarding than anything else that I have ever experienced as its pure life energy raises my quality of life given by improving my personal power to speak the truth of my inner real self with the ever-improving intuitive understanding of the higher intelligence. Being compassionately motivated down the rightful path, driven by personal power to thrive and help others as the inner self is encouraged to create the true image of real self-expression, I am intuitively given intelligent guidance for the highest potential of self and the outside world. Always constant, with quiet patience, the freely flowing life energy has been, is, and will continue to be the Universal Power, which is capable of working out everything for the highest good.

BIBLIOGRAPHY

Http://www.cdc.gov/des

Http://www.mercurypoisoned.com/symptoms.html

http://www.numerologywithatwist.com/sitebuilder/images/Chakra_Chart

http://www.lifeevents.org/5-tibetans-energy-rejuvenation-exercises.htm

http://www.mkprojects.com/pf_TibetanRites.htm

Dr. Karlis Ullis, Greg Ptacek. *Age right: turn back the clock with a proven personalized anti-aging program*. New York: Simon & Schuster, 1999.

Deepak Chopra, M.D. *Quantum Healing: exploring the frontiers of mind/body medicine*. New York: Bantam New Age Books, Division of Bantam Doubleday Dell publishing Group, Inc., 1989.

Deepak Chopra, M.D. *Creating Health: how to wake up the body's intelligence*. Boston: Houghton Mifflin Company, 1987.

Deepak Chopra, M.D. *Restful Sleep: the complete mind/body program for overcoming insomnia*. New York: Crown Trade Paperbacks, Member of the Crown Publishing Group, 1994.

Peter Kelder. *Ancient Secret of the Fountain of Youth, Book 2.* New York: Doubleday, Division of Random House, Inc., 1999(originally published by Gig Harbor, WA: Harbor Press, 1985).

Transport in cells: Active Transport/Cells/Biology/YouTube Fuse School

Davi-Ellen Chabner,B.A.,M.A.T. *The Language of Medicine, 7th Edition.* St. Louis, MO: Saunders, an Imprint of Elsevier, 2004.